Canada

by Kay Melchisedech Olson

Consultant:
Barry G. Ferguson, Ph.D.
Professor of History
University of Manitoba
Winnipeg, Canada

Blue Earth Books

an imprint of Capstone Press
Mankato, Minnesota

Blue Earth Books are published by Capstone Press,
151 Good Counsel Drive, P.O. Box 669, Mankato, Minnesota 56002.
www.capstonepress.com

Library of Congress Cataloging-in-Publication Data
Olson, Kay Melchisedech.
    Canada / by Kay Melchisedech Olson.
    v. cm.—(Many cultures, one world)
    Includes bibliographical references (p. 30) and index.
    Contents: Welcome to Canada—A Canadian legend—City and country life—Seasons in Canada—Family life in Canada—Laws, rules,
and customs—Pets in Canada—Sites to see in Canada.
    ISBN 0–7368–2166–X (hardcover)
    1. Canada—Juvenile literature. [1. Canada.] I. Title. II. Series.
F1008.2.045 2004
971—dc21   2002155262

Summary: An introduction to the geography, culture, and people of Canada, including a map, legend, recipe, craft, and game.

Editorial credits
Editor: Katy Kudela
Series Designer: Kia Adams
Photo Researcher: Alta Schaffer
Product Planning Editor: Karen Risch

Cover photo of Morraine Lake, by PhotoDisc Inc./Robert Glusic

Artistic effects
PhotoDisc

Capstone Press thanks Natalie Johnson, M.A., Assistant to the Director,
Institute for the Humanities, University of Manitoba, for her assistance
with this book.

2 3 4 5 6 08 07 06 05

Photo credits
Blaine Harrington III, 22–23
Bruce Coleman Inc./Erwin & Peggy Bauer, 10; Joe McDonald, 11
Capstone Press, 23 (bottom); Gary Sundermeyer, 3 (top right,
    middle, bottom), 15, 19, 21 (right), 25
Corbis/Gunter Marx Photography, 20–21
Houserstock/Dave G. Houser, 12–13, 13 (right), 16–17
Hulton/Archive Photos by Getty Images, 9
Larry Carver/The Viesti Collection Inc., 4–5
Maxine Cass, 28–29
Mervis and Lorie Groen, 27 (right)
One Mile Up Inc., 23 (top)
Sportees Activewear/Stephen Renyolds, 26–27
TRIP/A. Alborno, 14; BB Holdings BV, 6; N. Price, 24; W. Fraser, 17 (right), 18
West Edmonton Mall, 29 (right)

Contents

See page 7 to find a map of Canada.

Turn to page 15 to learn how to play a traditional Canadian game.

Look on page 19 to learn how to make a delicious Canadian dessert.

Check out page 25 to learn how to make a maple leaf sun catcher.

CHAPTER 1

Welcome to Canada

Canada is a country of unspoiled natural beauty. Forests stretch from border to border. Thousands of lakes, rivers, and streams flow through the landscape. Wild animals roam the wilderness.

Canadians and visitors enjoy many outdoor activities. Ice-skating and hockey are popular winter sports. Skiers enjoy gliding down snowy mountains.

People also enjoy Canada's natural areas in other seasons. Hunters and fishers come for

Tall mountains and green forests stretch across western Canada.

4

Facts about Canada

Name: ....Dominion of Canada

Capital: ....Ottawa

Population: ....31,414,000 people

Size: ....3,849,658 square miles

.........................(9,970,614 square kilometers)

Languages: ....English, French

Religions: ....Roman Catholicism,

.........................Protestantism, Judaism, Sikhism,

.........................Islam, Hinduism

Highest point: ...Mount Logan (Yukon Territory),

.........................19,550 feet (5,959 meters)

Lowest points: ..Arctic, Atlantic, and Pacific

.........................Oceans, sea level

Main crops: ....Wheat, fruit, vegetables

Money: ....Canadian dollar

the wild game. Campers and canoeists love the clean water and wilderness.

Canadians enjoy baseball and other summer sports. Lacrosse is the oldest sport played in Canada. Players use sticks with a pocket of netting. They try to carry and pass a hard rubber ball to each other. Canadians play lacrosse on a grassy field or in an arena.

People canoe on Lake Louise and other Canadian lakes.

Map of Canada

Legend
- ★ Capital City
- ● City
- ◆ Highest Point
- Mountain Range

GREENLAND

Mount Logan

YUKON TERRITORY

NORTHWEST TERRITORIES

TERRITORY OF NUNAVUT

BRITISH COLUMBIA

C A N A D A

A T L A N T I C

O C E A N

Hudson Bay

ALBERTA

Rocky Mountains

SASKATCHEWAN

MANITOBA

NEWFOUNDLAND AND LABRADOR

BANFF NATIONAL PARK

Badlands

ONTARIO

QUEBEC

NEW BRUNSWICK

PRINCE EDWARD ISLAND

P A C I F I C O C E A N

UNITED STATES

NOVA SCOTIA

Ottawa ★

Toronto ●

N
W   E
S

CHAPTER 2

A Canadian Legend

Altogether, Canada's six groups of native peoples speak 53 languages. The Inuit are one cultural and language group. At one time, they were called Eskimos. The Inuit were among the first people to live in Canada.

French explorers were the first permanent European settlers. During the early 1600s, they built homes and farms in an area they called New France.

Later, British soldiers captured New France. Great Britain then ruled that area of Canada.

During the 1900s, people from all over the world came to live in this big country. People with many different customs have shaped Canada's way of life. Folk stories are an important way of passing on customs to others.

One Canadian legend tells how the beaver and porcupine became enemies. Canada's folk stories often combine legends from different countries. Some legends have been passed down from native peoples. Legends often are based on fact but are not entirely true.

The Inuit were one of the first groups to settle in Canada. They continue to live along the Arctic coast and on Canada's northern islands.

Long ago in Canada, Beaver worked hard. He stored food for the coming winter. Porcupine played in the sun. He ignored the long, cold winter ahead.

One day while Beaver was out gathering food, Porcupine went to Beaver's house. He took all the food Beaver had been storing for winter. Beaver came home to find Porcupine had stolen his food.

Beaver was so angry he bit Porcupine. Porcupine's quills stuck all over Beaver's face. But Beaver held on tight to Porcupine. Beaver swam to an island in the middle of a lake. He pulled Porcupine along with him. Beaver then left Porcupine alone on the island.

Porcupine could not swim. He had no food. He was lonely and afraid. Porcupine cried himself to sleep. While he was asleep, Porcupine heard a voice say, "The North Wind can save you. Call the North Wind."

As loud as he could, Porcupine called the North Wind. He knew the North Wind brought cold weather. Porcupine knew he might freeze on the island during winter. Still, Porcupine asked the North Wind for help.

Beaver was a busy worker. He gathered food for the winter.

The North Wind answered Porcupine's calls. The weather got colder and colder. Soon ice covered the lake. Porcupine was able to walk across the ice to get off the island.

Now it was Porcupine's turn to be angry. He went to Beaver's house. While Beaver was asleep, Porcupine carried him to the top of a tall tree. He was sure Beaver could not climb down the tree. Porcupine thought Beaver would die in the tree.

When Beaver woke up, he saw he was up high in a tree. Beaver did not try to climb down. Instead, he began chewing the tree. He chewed and chewed. Soon he had chewed the tree down to a stump and was able to go home.

From that day on, beavers and porcupines have stayed away from one another. They remember what happened long ago between the first Beaver and Porcupine. That is how Beaver and Porcupine became enemies.

Porcupine was lazy. He liked to spend his time playing in the sun.

CHAPTER 3

City and Country Life

Most Canadians live in cities located within Canada's 10 provinces. Many people in cities live in single-family homes. Many others rent apartments.

Some Canadians live in Canada's three northern territories. These territories are wilderness areas. Fewer people live in the territories, but many animals make their homes in these large areas.

Children who live in Canada's countryside often live far from school.

Toronto is one of Canada's largest cities. Toronto is located in the Canadian province of Ontario.

Farms can be found in Canada's countryside.
Canadian farmers grow grains and raise livestock.

They must travel long distances by bus to get to class. Some children in faraway areas attend school at home. They do their lessons by computer.

In the country, Canadian farmers raise wheat and other grains. They also grow fruit, vegetables, and oilseeds. Many farmers raise cattle and other livestock.

Farmers in Canada use the country's rich soil to grow vegetables, grains, and fruit.

Play Bilboquet

Bilboquet (beel-boh-KAY) was a favorite game of both the Inuit people and the French Canadians. The game's name comes from the French. The word "bille" means "ball," and the word "bouquet" means "small piece of wood."

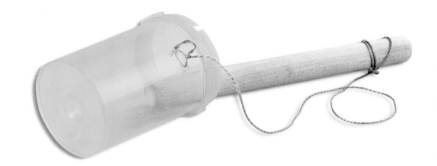

In this game, a ball or ring is attached by string to a stick. Holding onto the stick, a player flips up the ball or ring and tries to catch it with the handle. Inuit people used two types of animal bones to play this game. French Canadian children used a wooden stick and ball. You can make your own cup and stick.

What You Need

16-inch (50-centimeter) piece of string
dowel or unsharpened pencil
glue
small plastic cup

What You Do

1. Tie the string around the dowel or pencil.
2. Spread a little glue around the tied string end and set it aside to dry.
3. Ask an adult to drill holes in the plastic cup.
4. Tie the other end of the string around the holes in the cup.
5. See how many tries it takes to flip the cup up and catch it on the stick.

CHAPTER 4

Seasons in Canada

Canada's northern location affects its seasons. Winters in Canada are long and cold. Daylight hours are much fewer in winter. Canadian summer days are warm even in northern Canada. Summer daylight in northern Canada lasts nearly 20 hours.

Canada's short summer season is full of festivals. People celebrate the harvest of apples, strawberries, blueberries, and potatoes. They also hold seafood festivals. The Pictou Lobster Carnival marks the end of the lobster season in Nova Scotia.

Ice-skating is a favorite winter activity in Canada.

Apples are a main fruit crop in Canada. Canadians celebrate this important crop with summer festivals.

17

In July and August, the annual Sunflower, Corn, and Apple Festivals celebrate Canada's agriculture.

People celebrate the end of Canada's long winter with spring festivals. Maple syrup festivals are held in the eastern provinces of Ontario, Quebec, New Brunswick, and Nova Scotia. People enjoy sugaring-off parties. They cook maple sap until it thickens into syrup. In late spring, many provinces hold blossom festivals and parades.

Canadians also hold a tulip festival in Ottawa called the Festival of Spring. The royal family of the Netherlands sends thousands of tulip bulbs to Canada each year.

Frozen maple syrup is a favorite treat during spring festivals in Canada. Maple sap begins flowing in early spring.

Maple Syrup Pie

Canada's sugar maple trees produce millions of gallons of sap. In the early spring, people tap into the tree trunks. Sap drips from the trees and fills up buckets beneath the tap holes. People cook the sap until it thickens into syrup. This process is called sugaring-off. Many Canadians include maple syrup in recipes. Syrup pies have been popular in Canada since pioneer days.

What You Need

Ingredients
2 cups (480 mL) pure maple syrup
2 tablespoons (30 mL) butter
1 cup (240 mL) cold water
¼ cup (60 mL) cornstarch
1 egg
9-inch (23-centimeter) baked pie shell

Equipment
liquid-ingredient measuring cup
measuring spoons
small saucepan
empty jar (or container with tight lid)
dry-ingredient measuring cups
wire whisk

What You Do

1. Measure syrup and butter into saucepan and set aside.
2. Measure water and cornstarch into a jar. Close lid tightly and shake until contents are well blended and smooth.
3. Pour mixture into saucepan and stir.
4. Crack the egg into the empty jar. Replace lid and shake until egg is slightly beaten.
5. Add beaten egg to mixture in saucepan.
6. Cook over medium-low heat, stirring with a wire whisk until thick, about 7 minutes.
7. Remove saucepan from heat and pour mixture into baked pie shell.
8. Cool before serving.

Makes 6 slices

Family Life in Canada

Today, most families in Canada have one or two children. About 100 years ago, families of five or more children were common in Canada.

More than two-thirds of all Canadians live in houses. Many are two-story homes with bedrooms upstairs. Most have front and backyards.

About one-third of Canada's homes are apartments. Only a small number of apartments are in high-rise buildings.

Families in Canada enjoy outdoor activities. Dogsledding is a popular winter sport.

Birthdays in Canada

Canadian birthday parties include cake with a hidden surprise. Many birthday cakes have a foil-wrapped candy coin hidden between the layers. Whoever gets the piece with the candy coin is treated to a special honor. This person gets to take the first turn at all the party games.

Birthday crackers are a popular favor at Canadian birthday parties. A cracker is a small cardboard tube covered with colored paper. The crackers make a popping noise when opened. Small toys, candies, and goodies are hidden inside the cracker.

In Canada, the birthday child often has a shiny nose. First, people chase the birthday child. When caught, the child's nose gets rubbed with butter. This tradition is said to bring good luck. The birthday child's nose is too slippery for bad luck to stick.

CHAPTER 6

Laws, Rules, and Customs

Canada is an independent country. Ottawa is the capital of Canada's federal government. Canada has 10 provinces. Each of these statelike areas has its own capital. Canada also has three northern territories. These very large areas are governed by the national government.

Canada's national police force is called the Royal Canadian Mounted Police. People call the officers "Mounties." Mounties work to protect Canada's laws and people. Once, Mounties patrolled

The Royal Canadian Mounted Police often appear on horseback during parades and festivals. During their workday, most Mounties travel in police cars.

Canada's national flag is red and white. A large red maple leaf sits on the white center. The maple leaf is Canada's national emblem. The red in Canada's flag stands for France. The white color stands for England.

Canada's money is called the dollar. One hundred cents equal one dollar. Canadian dollars come in paper bills and coins. The $1 coin has a picture of a loon. People call it a "loony." They call the $2 coin a "two-ny."

large areas of Canada on horseback. Today, most Mounties travel in police cars.

Each of Canada's provinces makes its own rules about schools. Most children in Canada must begin school by age 5. Depending on the province where they live, children finish high school between ages 15 and 18. Students learn both of Canada's languages, English and French. They may also study other languages.

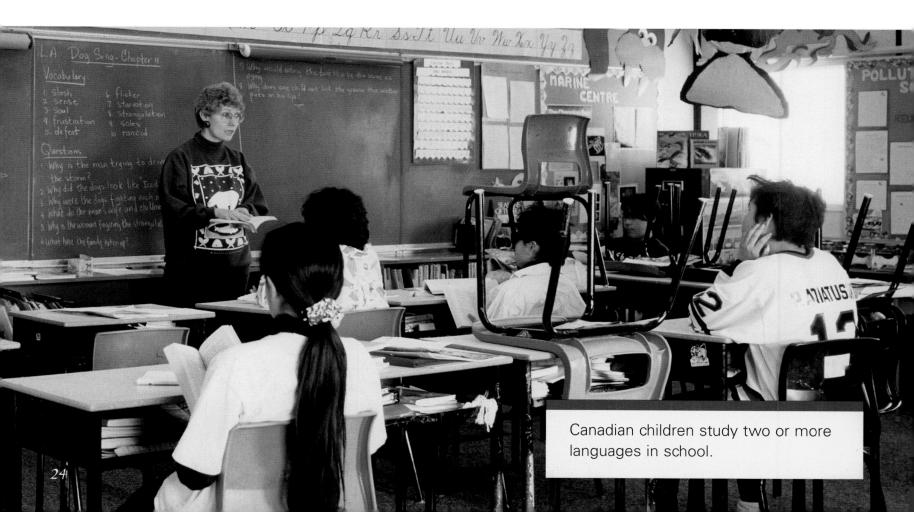

Canadian children study two or more languages in school.

Maple Leaf Sun Catcher

The maple leaf is Canada's national emblem. There are 125 known species of maple trees in the world. Only 13 maple species are native to North America. Ten of these 13 species grow in Canada. At least one of these 10 species of maples grows naturally in every province of Canada.

What You Need

one red maple leaf (natural leaf or cut from red construction paper)
waxed paper (2 sheets)
paper towel (2 sheets)
clothes iron
scissors
hole punch
yarn

What You Do

1. Collect a red maple leaf. Or, cut the shape of a maple leaf from red construction paper.
2. Put the leaf between two sheets of waxed paper.
3. Put the two sheets of waxed paper between two sheets of paper towel.
4. With an adult's help, turn a clothes iron to the highest setting.
5. Gently iron over the top paper towel. Make sure the iron passes over each area of the paper towel.
6. Let the paper towel cool to the touch. The waxed paper should be stuck together around the leaf.
7. With scissors, trim the waxed paper around the leaf.
8. Punch a hole at the top with a hole punch.
9. Thread yarn through the hole and tie into a loop.
10. Hang the sun catcher in a sunny window.

CHAPTER 7

Pets in Canada

Almost half the homes in Canada have a pet. Cats, dogs, and horses are popular pets in Canada. People once kept dogs and horses to do work. These animals carried packs and helped hunters look for food.

All Canadians share their land, water, and air with many other creatures. About 200 different species of mammals live in Canada. The country has more than 425 species of birds and 950 kinds of fish. Canada is also home to 55,000 known kinds of insects and 82 kinds of amphibians.

Many children in Canada have a pet dog.

Canadian Dogs

Several dog breeds began in Canada. The Newfoundland dog (below) was first bred in the province of Newfoundland. These dogs are good swimmers. The Nova Scotia duck toller was first bred in southern Nova Scotia. This dog tricks ducks into coming closer to the hunter.

27

CHAPTER 8

Sites to See in Canada

Visitors come to Canada for its forests, clear lakes, and other natural wonders. A mountain range in western Canada is known as the Canadian Rockies. Banff National Park in Alberta is known for its beautiful scenery and wild animals.

Alberta's Red Deer River Valley has strange rock formations called hoodoos. Many people visit Canada's Badlands to see the hoodoos.

Rock formations called hoodoos are an interesting site to see in Canada's Red Deer River Valley.

World's Largest Shopping Center

Canada's West Edmonton Mall is the world's largest entertainment and shopping center. Visitors can ride the world's largest indoor triple-loop roller coaster. They also can shop in more than 800 stores without going outdoors.

Canada's West Edmonton Mall features the world's largest indoor lake.

Words to Know

beaver (BEE-vur)—an animal with a wide, flat tail; beavers live both on land and in water.

emblem (EM-bluhm)—a symbol or a sign

Inuit (IN-oo-it)—a person, or a group of people, from the Arctic region of Canada

lacrosse (luh-KRAWSS)—a ball game for two teams in which each player has a long stick with a small netted pocket on the end; players use the pocket to hold, pass, or throw the ball to one another.

oilseed (OIL-seed)—a seed or crop grown mainly for its oil

porcupine (POR-kyuh-pine)—a small animal covered with long, sharp quills that are used for protection

province (PROV-uhnss)—a territory containing a unit of government within a nation; Canada is made up of provinces.

species (SPEE-sheez)—a group of plants or animals with similar features

To Learn More

Bowers, Vivien. *Wow, Canada!: Exploring this Land from Coast to Coast to Coast.* Toronto: Owl Books, 1999.

Costain, Meredith, and Paul Collins. *Welcome to Canada.* Countries of the World. Philadelphia: Chelsea House, 2002.

Gray, Shirley W. *Canada.* First Reports. Minneapolis: Compass Point Books, 2000.

Koestler-Grack, Rachel A. *The Inuit: Ivory Carvers of the Far North.* America's First Peoples. Mankato, Minn.: Blue Earth Books, 2004.

Useful Addresses

Canadian Children's Museum
P.O. Box 3100, Station B
100 Laurier Street
Gatineau, Quebec J8X 4H2
Canada

Canadian Embassy
501 Pennsylvania Avenue NW
Washington, DC 20001

Canadian Tourism Commission
55 Metcalfe Street, Suite 600
Ottawa, Ontario K1P 6L5
Canada

National Library of Canada
395 Wellington Street
Ottawa, Ontario K1A 0N4
Canada

Internet Sites

Do you want to find out more about Canada?
Let FactHound, our fact-finding hound dog, do the research for you.

Here's how:

1) Visit *http://www.facthound.com*
2) Type in the **Book ID** number: **073682166X**
3) Click on **FETCH IT.**

FactHound will fetch Internet sites picked by our editors just for you!

Index